Fact Cat

CONTINENTS

Izzi Howell

D1529912

WAYLAND

FACT CAT

Get your paws on this fantastic new mega-series from Wayland!

Join our Fact Cat on a journey of fun learning about every subject under the sun!

Published in paperback in 2016 by Wayland
Copyright © Wayland 2016

ISBN: 978 0 7502 9027 2
Library ebook ISBN: 978 0 7502 9026 5
Dewey Number: 910.9'141-dc23

10 9 8 7 6 5 4 3 2 1

MIX
Paper from responsible sources
FSC® C104740

Wayland
An imprint of Hachette Children's Group
Part of Hodder & Stoughton
Carmelite House
50 Victoria Embankment
London EC4Y 0DZ

An Hachette UK Company
www.hachette.co.uk
www.hachettechildrens.co.uk

A catalogue for this title is available from the British Library
Printed and bound in China

Produced for Wayland by
White-Thomson Publishing Ltd
www.wtpub.co.uk
+44 (0) 843 208 7460

Editor: Izzi Howell
Design: Rocket Design (East Anglia) Ltd
Fact Cat illustrations: Shutterstock/Julien Troneur
Other illustrations: Stefan Chabluk
Consultant: Kate Ruttle

Picture and illustration credits:
Dreamstime: Artur Bogacki 5, Perati Komson 13, Johncarnemolla 14cr, Dmitry Pichugin 15, Daniel Cota 20b; Shutterstock: Anton Balazh cover and title page, saiko3p 6, Mark Schwettmann 7, ZRyzner 8b, WitR 9, Volodymyr Goinyk 10b, erwinf. 11b, Kristian Bell 14bl, andYLand 16b, leoks 17, holbox 18b, tipograffias 19, meunierd 21t, Catarina Belova 21b; Stefan Chabluk 4; Thinkstock: Elenarts 8t, 10t, Fuse 11t, Elenarts 12t, Danielrao 12b, Elenarts 14tl, Yahya Idiz 14cl, Andras Deak 14br, Elenarts 16t, 18t, 20t.

Every effort has been made to clear copyright.
Should there be any inadvertent omission,
please apply to the publisher for rectification.

The author, Izzi Howell, is a writer and editor specialising in children's educational publishing.

The consultant, Kate Ruttle, is a literacy expert and SENCO, and teaches in Suffolk.

FACT CAT FACT

There is a question for you to answer on each spread in this book. You can check your answers on page 24.

CONTENTS

WHAT IS A CONTINENT?

A continent is a very large area of land and any **surrounding** islands. There are seven continents on Earth – Africa, Antarctica, Asia, Australasia and Oceania, Europe, North America and South America.

Some continents are joined to each other, such as Asia and Europe. Look at the map and find two other continents that are joined together.

North America

Europe

Asia

Africa

equator

South America

Australasia and Oceania

Antarctica

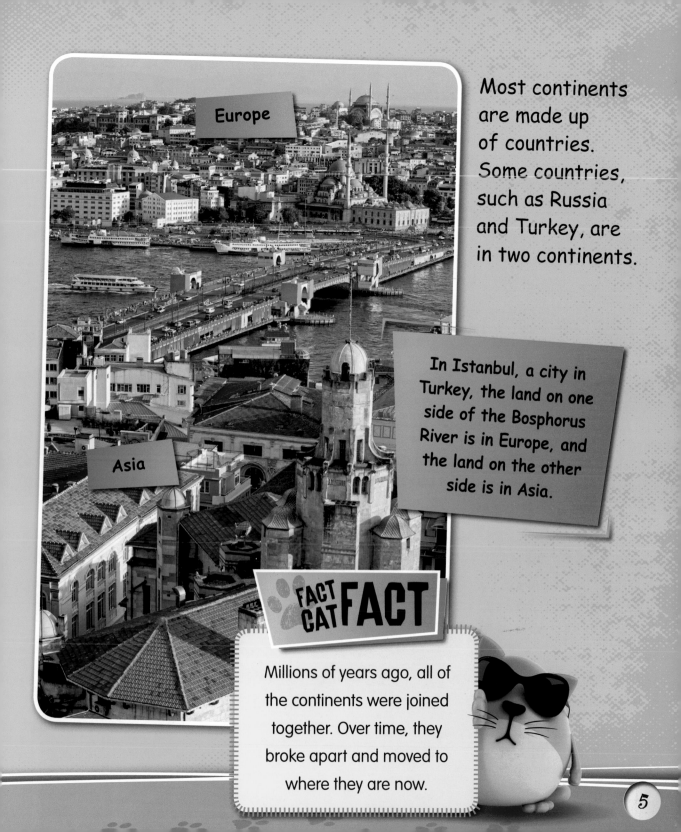

Europe

Asia

Most continents are made up of countries. Some countries, such as Russia and Turkey, are in two continents.

In Istanbul, a city in Turkey, the land on one side of the Bosphorus River is in Europe, and the land on the other side is in Asia.

FACT CAT FACT

Millions of years ago, all of the continents were joined together. Over time, they broke apart and moved to where they are now.

POPULATION AND SIZE

The **population** of a continent is the number of people that live there. Asia has the highest population of any continent. More than 4 **billion** people live there.

This colourful market stall is in India, a country in Asia.

Asia is also the biggest continent by size. It covers more than 44 million square kilometres, which is almost a third of all land on Earth. The second biggest continent is Africa.

Australasia and Oceania is the smallest continent by size. Many of its countries are islands in the Pacific Ocean. Find out the names of two Pacific islands.

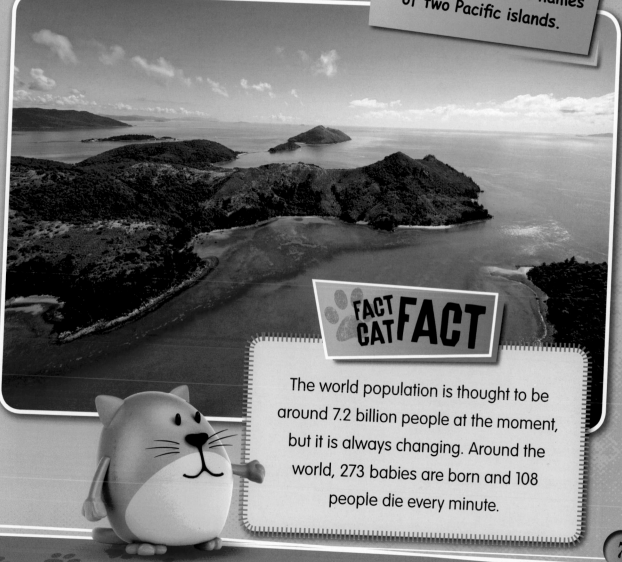

FACT CAT FACT

The world population is thought to be around 7.2 billion people at the moment, but it is always changing. Around the world, 273 babies are born and 108 people die every minute.

AFRICA

There are rainforests in the middle of Africa, along the **equator**. The equator passes through seven African countries. Find out the names of three of them.

To the north and the south of the equator is **savannah**, **dry** areas where grass and some trees grow. The Maasai are a group of people that live on the savannah.

More than one billion people live in Africa's 54 countries. In the north, Africa is joined to Asia by a small piece of land.

Africa is home to the Nile, the longest river in the world. It flows for almost 6,900 km near the east coast of the continent.

FACT CAT FACT

The world's fastest land animal, the cheetah, lives in Africa. Cheetahs can run as fast as a car can drive – up to 114 kilometres per hour!

 # ANTARCTICA

Antarctica is surrounded by the Southern Ocean. The South Pole is near the centre of Antarctica.

A thick layer of ice covers nearly all of the surface of Antarctica. There are no trees or grass. Find out what kind of plants grow in Antarctica.

FACT CAT FACT

Antarctica is the coldest continent, with temperatures reaching -89 °C. Water freezes at 0 °C , and most freezers are -18 °C, so it's difficult to imagine just how cold Antarctica is.

Although nobody lives in Antarctica all year round, scientists and tourists do visit. Scientists stay for a few months to do experiments. Tourists come on cruises for a few days to take photographs.

Emperor penguins live in Antarctica.

research base

In the summer, there are up to 4,000 scientists living and working on **research bases** in Antarctica.

ASIA

In **inland** areas of Asia, the weather is dry. Along the southeast coast, the weather is hot and wet.

From June to September, heavy rains, called monsoons, fall in southeast Asia. These can cause **floods**.

More than half of the population of Asia live in just two of its countries – China and India. The rest of its population is divided between 47 other countries.

Tokyo, the **capital** of Japan, is the biggest city in the world. Over 37 million people live there, which is more than the population of Australasia and Oceania.

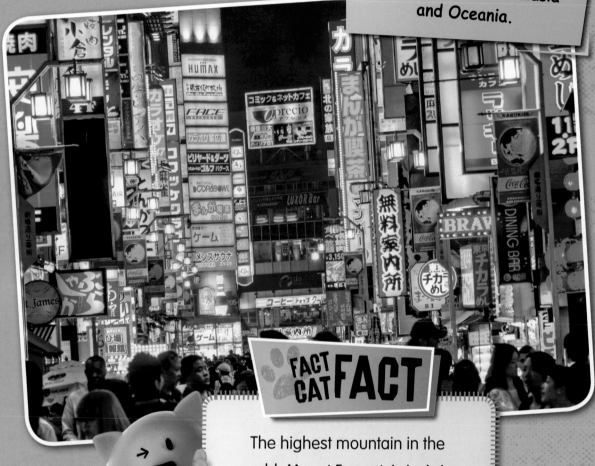

FACT CAT FACT

The highest mountain in the world, Mount Everest, is in Asia. It is found in a **mountain range** called the Himalayas. Find out the height of Mount Everest.

AUSTRALASIA AND OCEANIA

After Antarctica, Australasia and Oceania has the lowest population. Only 36 million people live in its 14 countries.

kangaroo

platypus

These animals are **native** to Australia. They don't live anywhere else in the world. Find out the name of another native Australian animal.

echidna

koala

In the south of the continent, the weather is mild in the islands of New Zealand. The winters are cool and the summers are hot. Wellington, the capital of New Zealand, is the southernmost capital city in the world.

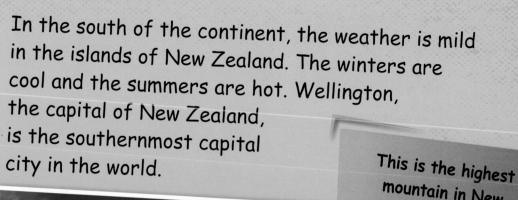

This is the highest mountain in New Zealand. Aoraki is its **Maori** name and Mount Cook is its English name.

FACT CAT FACT

There are so many sheep farms in New Zealand that the country has a population of 40 million sheep and only 4.5 million people.

EUROPE

Even though Europe is the second smallest continent by size, it has 50 countries and a population of 740 million people. To the east, Europe has a long **border** with Asia.

The Eiffel Tower is one of the most visited attractions in the world. Find out which European city it is in.

This village is on the Mediterranean coast. The houses are painted white to keep them cool.

There are lots of woodland areas in the north of Europe. The south of Europe is dry, with mountains along the Mediterranean Sea.

FACT CAT FACT

The smallest country in the world by size and population is in Europe. Vatican City is about the same size as 37 football pitches. Only 842 people live there, including the **Pope**.

# NORTH AMERICA

There are 23 countries in North America. Some are very big, such as the USA and Canada, and some are small, such as the island of Haiti.

The Horseshoe Bend is a natural **curve** in the Colorado River. It is found in the southwest of the USA.

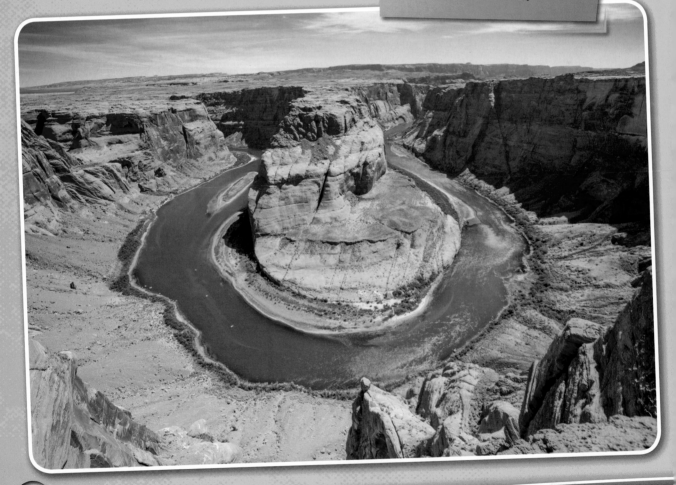

North America is the third largest continent by size and population. Around 528 million people live there.

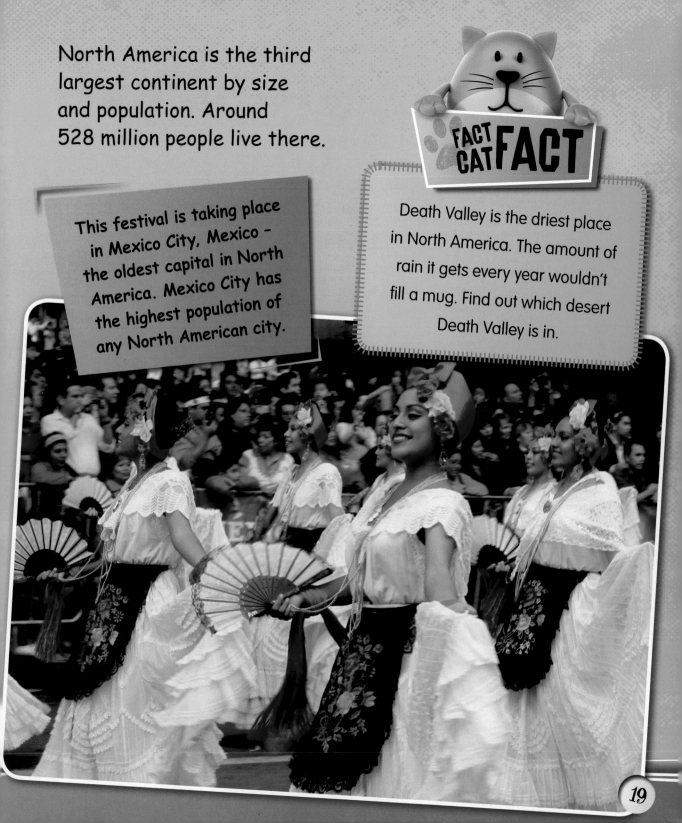

FACT CAT FACT

This festival is taking place in Mexico City, Mexico – the oldest capital in North America. Mexico City has the highest population of any North American city.

Death Valley is the driest place in North America. The amount of rain it gets every year wouldn't fill a mug. Find out which desert Death Valley is in.

SOUTH AMERICA

There are 12 countries in South America. Over 370 million people live there. It is joined to North America by a small piece of land.

Iguazu Falls is made up of 275 separate waterfalls. Find out which two South American countries it is in.

FACT CAT FACT

Fried guinea pig is a popular dish in Peru and Bolivia. Some people say it tastes like chicken!

The weather in the north is hot and wet. People go to Copacabana Beach in Brazil to enjoy the sunshine. In the south, there can be snow on the high Andes mountains.

Copacabana Beach

llama

These children live in the Andes. Their llama helps them to carry heavy things up the mountains.

Try to answer the questions below. Look back through the book to help you. Check your answers on page 24.

1 How many people live in Asia?

a) 2 billion
b) 4 billion
c) 6 billion

2 What is the longest river in the world?

a) the Nile
b) the Thames
c) the Ganges

3 Scientists work in Antarctica in the summer. True or not true?

a) true
b) not true

4 Shanghai is the biggest city in the world. True or not true?

a) true
b) not true

5 Europe has a border with Asia. True or not true?

a) true
b) not true

6 How many countries are in North America?

a) 12
b) 19
c) 23